M000092536

Frédéric Chopin
Three Mazurkas

Edited by
Randall Faber

Production: Frank and Gail Hackinson
Production Coordinator: Marilyn Cole
Cover: Terpstra Design, San Francisco
Engraving: GrayBear Music Company, Hollywood, Florida
Printer: Tempo Music Press, Inc.

ISBN 978-1-61677-153-9

ABOUT THE SERIES

THE COMPOSER collections in the *Keyboard Artist Library* present three or four related pieces by a single composer. In studying several pieces from a select part of the keyboard literature, a pianist learns much about a composer's style and a particular musical form. A depth of understanding and musical meaning accompanies this concentrated study. These composer collections make such focused study manageable and affordable. They are carefully edited for accuracy and instructional value. Pieces are presented in approximate order of difficulty.

Study Suggestions

- Listen to recordings, learn the opening of each piece,
    then select the piece you would like to learn first.
- Study all three pieces. Then memorize your favorite, or favorites.
- Compare the recordings of several different pianists.

CONTENTS

Thanks and acknowledgment to George Kooistra
for his assistance in research and text editing.

FRÉDÉRIC CHOPIN (1810-1849)

CHOPIN has been called the reluctant romantic.* Although he deplored the term, Chopin was indeed the preeminent romantic composer of his time. Born into a middle-class family in a small village outside of Warsaw, Poland, he became the toast of Paris after his piano debut there at age twenty-one. Chopin's father was French, his mother Polish. And though he expressed a passionate devotion to Poland, he never returned to his homeland after he left in 1830.

As the third child in the family, young Frédéric was drawn to the piano playing of his mother and older sister. He began his piano studies at age six, and composed a Polonaise in B-flat at age seven! At the same age, his G-minor Polonaise was published and hailed as a work of genius. Years later Robert Schumann in reviewing the publication of one of Chopin's early compositions wrote: "Hats off, Gentlemen, a genius."

Chopin's first teacher, Adalbert Zwyny, inspired him with a special devotion to the keyboard music of J. S. Bach. At age twelve he began composition studies with Joseph Elsner, then head of the Warsaw Conservatory. Chopin entered the conservatory as a regular student at the age of sixteen and graduated three years later. Again, he was called "a musical genius" by Elsner.

In 1829 Chopin traveled with friends to Vienna where he presented two concert performances of his own works. While there he met Czerny, who expressed admiration for the young pianist. After travel to Prague and Dresden, Chopin returned to his home in Warsaw where he gave three concerts before leaving again in November 1830. He performed again in Vienna, and later in Munich. From there he traveled to Stuttgart and finally to Paris where he arrived to stay in September of 1831.

Following his Paris debut, Chopin presented other concerts; but he disliked public performances. He preferred instead to play in the private salons of his wealthy patrons. Chopin became a sought-after house guest of fashionable Parisian society, attracting many students from the aristocracy. He socialized freely among the French intellectual elite, and numbered among his friends and acquaintances the celebrated musicians, writers, and painters of his time.

Chopin died at the early age of 39. Yet, during his brief lifetime he composed more than 200 compositions for piano. Many of these pieces have remained in the performing repertoire of concert pianists worldwide—nearly a century-and-a-half since their introduction to European music lovers. Chopin's music has also endeared him to countless non-professional pianists, especially those whom C. P. E. Bach termed "connoisseurs and amateurs." For, along with the virtuoso etudes and other technically demanding works, Chopin also composed many pieces that are within the technical grasp of serious intermediate pianists.

This reluctant romantic—perhaps the greatest of them all—despised overly sentimental playing. His taste was founded on the music of Bach and Mozart. So, while Chopin's music is known for its poetic charm and emotional appeal, it also demands the utmost clarity and rhythmic accuracy.

---

*Jeremy Siepmann, *Chopin: The Reluctant Romantic* (Boston: Northeastern University Press, 1995).

ABOUT THE MAZURKAS

CHOPIN wrote 57 mazurkas from age fourteen to his last year, 47 of them published during his lifetime. After Chopin's death, his boyhood friend and fellow pianist Jules Fontana published the other ten mazurkas taken from Chopin's manuscripts (even though the composer thought them unworthy of printing). Taken together, the mazurkas constitute the most personal, refined, and original of Chopin's creations. They could be said to be musical caviar for the connoisseur.

The late 19th-century American music critic James Huneker called the mazurkas "Dances of the Soul." Extremely varied, they can be lyrical, contrapuntal, dramatic, whimsical, melancholy, chromatic or modal. At times they assume the coloring of other instruments—the drone of a bagpipe in the middle section of Op. 7, No. 1, for instance.

The mazurka originally took its name from the Mazur people of the province of Mazovia, Chopin's birthplace. It was one of a number of folk dances known by the generic term *oborek*, a turning dance for couples. Included in the mazurka category are three types: the *kujawiak*, a slow and serious dance; the *mazur*, in moderate tempo; and the *obertas*, fastest of the three. The melancholy *kujawiak* is usually in a minor mode, often with raised fourth and lowered seventh scale degrees. Dotted rhythms and wide leaps are characteristic of the faster *mazur* and *obertas*. These three types of mazurka dances are represented in the three contrasting mazurkas of this collection.

Triplet figures, weak-beat accents, and grace notes are often seen in the mazurkas. These are short art pieces based on the dance, but suitable for performance in private salons and other intimate surroundings. Chopin himself remarked of his first set of published mazurkas, Op. 6, "They are not for dancing."

Some of Chopin's early mazurkas struck his conservative contemporaries as novel and strange. They were shocked by his daring harmonies; startled by the sharp dissonances and unexpected digressions. Chains of dominant sevenths or diminished sevenths often lend splashes of exotic color to the mazurkas, and tend to counteract the regularity of triple-time dance meter.

The mazurkas are miniature "tone poems" that often contain breathtaking harmonic turns, yet hold to the formal structure of the dance. In these compositions Chopin elevated the mazurka to an art form, combining the rustic flavor of the Polish dance with the elegance and sophistication of the French salon.

PERFORMANCE NOTES

Mazurka in F Major (Op. 68, No. 3) Consider this piece a study in contrasts. The fanfare opening is echoed by the eight measures that follow. Then a four-measure *ff* statement is echoed with a four-measure *p* response. The tempo of the *mazur* (see above) is broken with a slightly hurried, though playful, section on the subdominant (the IV chord). Notice the pedal effect for this passage, which should be observed.

Mazurka in G Minor (Op. 67, No. 2) In the style of the *kujawiak*, this contemplative piece requires careful listening and a restrained tempo. Contrast the extroversion of the B section with the introspective opening and with the *sotto voce* (very soft, "under the voice") passage that follows. Notice the *mf* dynamic at the return, which suggests a more confident final presentation of the melody.

Mazurka in B-flat Major (Op. 7, No. 1) The wild and carefree spirit of the *obertas* is evident in the opening three bars. The rhythmic scale makes a bold crescendo as it ascends from the dominant to tonic scale steps. As if transformed by the trill, the melody suddenly turns soft with playful leaps over the I and V7 harmonies. The performer may vary this dynamic contrast later in the piece, moving the *subito piano* dynamic to the last four measures of the section (*mm. 41* and *61*). The *sotto voce* section features an exotic B-flat minor melody with a raised 4th over a bagpipe drone. Though marked for a long pedal, use quick pedal changes to reduce the accumulating resonance on the modern piano.

Mazurka in F Major

Op. 68, No. 3
(composed in 1829)

Allegro ma non troppo (♩ = 132)

a) The 𝄑 ❊ notations show the composer's pedal markings. The graphic pedal indications (⌐————∧————⌐) are editorial.

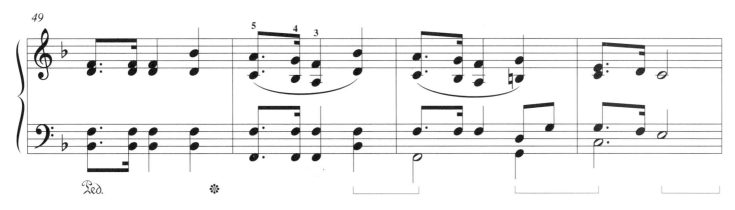

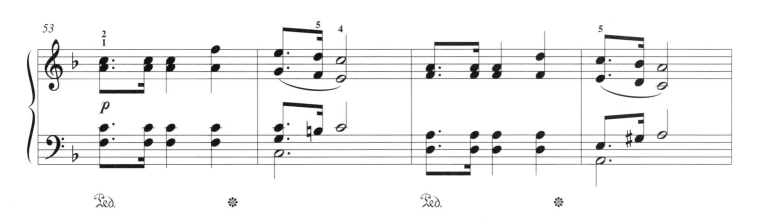

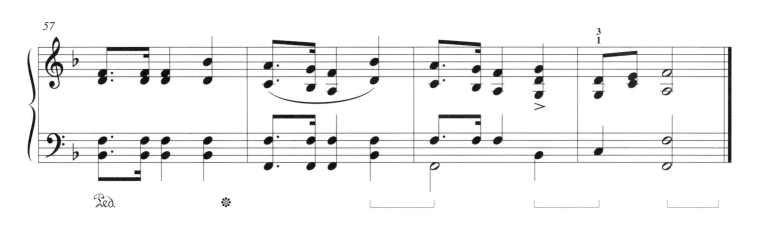

Mazurka in G Minor

Cantabile (♩ = 144)

Op. 67, No. 2
(composed in 1849)

a) The performer should feel free to use frequent and subtle changes of pedal.
b) The phrasing in this mazurka is editorial.

c) The grace note should be played *sforzando* and on the beat.
d) The graphic pedal indications are editorial.
e) Bring out the alto voice through m. 28.

f) If you can reach the 10th, hold the bass note and pedal on beat 2.

to Monsieur Johns of New Orleans

Mazurka in B-flat Major

Op. 7, No. 1
(composed in 1830/1831)

Vivace (♩. = 50)

a) This trill is most effective beginning on the upper note.

b) Try playing the grace notes on the beat.

c) Similarly for other trills (⌇ or *tr*)

FF1153

14

d) The pedal indications here are editorial. All 🎵 ❋ notations show the composer's pedal markings.

FF1153

e) Most editions show a staccato mark for the B♭. If played staccato, the note should be pedalled.
f) This ornament is played the same as in m. 46.
g) Try using $\frac{1}{5}$ fingering on the accented 5th.

DICTIONARY OF MUSICAL TERMS

allegro	Fast (Literally, it means "cheerful.")
a tempo	Resume the earlier tempo.
cantabile	Singing, or as if singing
crescendo (cresc.)	Get gradually louder.
e	And (Italian). For example, *cresc e rit.*
forzando (fz)	Forced, accented; same as *sforzando*
legatissimo	Very legato, almost overlapping
ma non troppo	But not too much
mazurka	See page 3.
opus (Op.)	Work. A composer's compositions are often arranged in sequence, and each work given an *opus* number. Several pieces may be included in a single opus: Op. 3, No. 1; Op. 3, No. 2; etc.
𝄽𝄾.	An authentic mark meaning depress the damper pedal
✳	An authentic mark indicating the release of the damper pedal
più	More. For example, *più cresc.* means more crescendo.
poco	A little
rallentando (rall.)	A gradual slowing of speed; same as *ritardando*
ritardando (rit.)	A gradual slowing of speed; same as *rallentando*
ritenuto (riten.)	A sudden slowing of speed
rubato	An expressive give and take in the tempo
scherzando	Playful and light; like a *scherzo*
sforzando (sf or sfz)	A sudden strong accent
simile	Similarly; continue in the same manner (same pedaling, same use of staccato, etc.)
sotto voce	Literally, "under the voice"; very soft
stretto	Chopin used this term to indicate more forward motion; a slight, forward push of the tempo.
Tempo I	Resume the tempo of the first section.
trill (tr or ⁓)	A quick repetition of the principal note with the note above it. (The number and speed of the repetitions depend on the situation.)
una corda	Depress the soft pedal. (literally means, "one string")
vivace	Quick and lively
vivo	Fast, with life